ECONOMICS IN A NUTSHELL

THIRTY THINGS THAT WILL HELP YOU UNDERSTAND THE SOCIAL SCIENCE OF ECONOMICS

—⁕—

BY

DR. BRADLEY W. RASCH

TABLE OF CONTENTS

—ɯ—

INTRODUCTION

Merriam-Webster defines Economics in the following manner: A Social science that analyzes and describes the consequences of choices made concerning scarce productive resources. Economics is the study of how individuals and societies choose to employ those resources: what goods and services will be produced, how they will be produced, and how they will be distributed among the members of society. Economics is customarily divided into microeconomics and macroeconomics. Of major concern to macroeconomists are the rate of economic growth, the inflation rate, and the rate of unemployment. Specialized areas of economic investigation attempt to answer questions on a variety of economic activity; they include agricultural economics, economic development, economic history, environmental economics, industrial organization, international trade, labor economics, money supply and banking, public finance, urban economics, and welfare economics. Specialists in mathematical economics and econometrics provide tools used by all economists. The areas of investigation in economics overlap with many other disciplines, notably history, mathematics, political science, and sociology.

Perhaps a simpler definition is: **Economics** is the social science that studies economic activity to gain an understanding of the processes that govern the production, distribution and consumption of goods and services in an economy.

Tyler Cown once said:
Economics is everywhere, and understanding economics can help you make better decisions and lead a happier life.

Sam Harris stated: Human well-being is not a random phenomenon. It depends on many factors - ranging from genetics and neurobiology to sociology and economics. But, clearly, there are scientific truths to be known about how we can flourish in this world. Wherever we can have an impact on the well being of others, questions of morality apply.

None other than John Kenneth Galbraith opined: Economics is extremely useful as a form of employment for economists.

Economics in a Nutshell endeavors to provide the reader with a high degree of literacy in the important and interesting discipline of Economics. We shall try to supply your demand for information about this fascinating discipline.

1

SUPPLY AND DEMAND

Supply and demand are such important concepts in Economics that the Scottish philosopher Thomas Carlyle (1795-1881) famously said, "Teach a parrot the terms 'supply and demand' and you've got an Economist." Though Economics cannot be simplified to this extent, Carlyle's comment is an excellent tongue and cheek underscoring of the importance of these two concepts to the understanding of Economics.

The law of supply and demand explains why some things cost so much more than others. An affordable long lasting watch will sell for a reasonable amount of money. A premium watch, with an impressive brand name, that also tells time, will sell for considerably more money. Why? In part, because there are fewer of these premium luxury watches (supply) and many people are seeking this watch of status (demand).

You may be willing to purchase a bottle of water at a gas station for two dollars. It is one of hundreds of bottles they have chilling and waiting for you at the service station. That same bottle of water offered to you by a man you meet while walking across the desert, miles from your broken down car, may fetch $20.

The examples of the watch and the water allow us to understand the relationships between supply, demand, and price.

In days long gone, one could purchase about anything from a stall on Maxwell Street in Chicago at the weekend market. You can also purchase stocks from the New York Stock Exchange. Both are markets, places where things are bought and sold, and both are subject to the laws of supply and demand.

A market is a place or experience that allows buyers and sellers to interact. It can happen over the Internet or at a physical marketplace. Supply, demand, and price are relevant to all markets, and each of these things tells us a great deal about what is valued in a society.

Demand is simply the amount of a tangible item, or service, someone is willing to purchase from a seller at a specific price. As a general rule, the higher the price, the fewer buyers there will be. Supply is the amount of a product (or service) a seller will offer you at a specific price. If prices are low, the seller is not motivated to make a lot of an item for sale, or to provide a lot of a service, because making an item or providing a service takes money and time.

Price tells us if supply or demand for an item is rising or falling. There are a lot of people that want to buy homes in North Dakota (huge demand) and not enough homes available to meet the needs of people that want to live in North Dakota (low supply). Thus, houses are very expensive, especially compared to the price of homes in North Dakota before massive amounts of oil were discovered, and thousands of oil related jobs became available.

When homes can be sold in an area at good prices, and builders can make big profits building them, they will build more houses in that specific area. They will not build large numbers of homes in other areas where people do not want to live. When the economy went bad in Detroit, very few people wanted to move there. Detroit was loosing jobs. Because there were so many houses available for sale, and virtually no one looking to buy a home in Detroit, homes could be purchased at absurdly low prices.

You can go to your local florist and purchase a rose for a dollar in September, and make some points with your loved one. That same rose will cost you five dollars February 14. Why? There is more demand for roses on Valentines Day, more people want them. Also, in the dead of winter, there may be fewer roses available. Supply, demand, and price, are all related.

Sometimes prices determined by demand are an indication of consumer preference that is interesting. Take a car, for example. It may come in red, green, or black. The cars are identical except for the color. Red, green, or black cars are available in large supply. They can all be had for the same or very similar price. But lets say the manufacturer offers a very limited number of that same exact car in a really cool and trendy shade of yellow. Consumers may snatch up this limited edition car for 500 or 600 more dollars than the red, green, or black models even though the cars are identical except for color. People are often willing to pay more for something in short supply that allows them to stand out from their friends.

Fluctuations in supply and demand will change prices of a good or service, but not necessarily immediately. If your cable TV company starts charging you more, you may downgrade to a cheaper package, or even give up cable and subscribe to satellite TV. The term for this tendency is elastic demand. In other words, if something goes up in price, we may buy less of it, or stop buying it all together. Some demand then is *price elastic.*

Sometimes we are slow to or unwilling to change our behavior when prices go up. Gas prices go up at the pump. We still have to drive to work, drive to the store. We cannot cut down on our driving, or our gas purchases. When this happens, it is said that we consumers are price inelastic.

Supply can also be elastic or inelastic. An elastic business may lay off workers when consumers want to buy fewer of their products. Some businesses may not lay off workers and keep producing when prices are low, their response would be considered inelastic.

If you are a whittler, and can whittle beautiful figurines for tourists, if you are good you can make a living. You are not going to sell these figurines for $5 because you have to rent a stall at the local market, and, even though people would line up and buy them all day long for $5, you cannot sell them at that price because you will not make any money. If you sell the figurines at $50 a piece, very few if any people would buy your handicraft, and you would not be able to pay your overhead. You might find that if you set the price at $12 an item, you will sell enough to meet overhead and make a profit. There are enough people willing to buy your crafts at that price for you to sell a reasonable number of them. Sometimes, a little experimentation is necessary to find out at what price an item will bring in a steady amount of business. A supply and demand curve can be plotted for any item. If you put price on a vertical axis, and amount of an item made on the horizontal axis, where the two lines meet would become the equilibrium price, the price at which items should sell well and the producer can make a decent profit.

In 1776 Adam Smith wrote *The Wealth of Nations,* and discussed at length the relationships between supply, demand, and price. In the 1930's John Hicks (1904-1989), a British Economist wrote extensively about supply, demand, and price.

2

OPPORTUNITY COSTS

Could your time or money be better spent doing something else? This question is a great introduction to the economic concept of opportunity costs.

We only have so much time in a day. There are always many things we can do during a given time period. But we can only do one thing at a time. When we are at work working we cannot be watching our favorite show or fishing. So when we are working, we are probably missing out on opportunities to do things we may enjoy more. This is an opportunity cost.

Going to college (and earning a degree) is certainly an excellent idea and investment for most people. Your lifetime earnings will be higher, and you will have become a better educated and more well rounded person. But those four or five years you spent full time in college have opportunity costs. Four years of no income. The time you spent in college, and the earnings you missed out on are opportunity costs. As this book is being written, for some people, the opportunity costs associated with missing out on four years of employment by attending college may be a bit more significant than they have been in the past. This is because good jobs can be hard to come by, even for college graduates. All and all, it is still better *long term*, to have a college diploma.

Businesses as well as people encounter opportunity costs. If you own a factory that makes automobile tires and you invest $10,0000,00 in a machine that increases your tire production, it may be money well spent. You could also have invested that $10,0000,000 in a bank account, stocks, or bonds. Let us say that ten million dollar investment placed in a savings account could earn you $500,000 a year in interest. That half a million dollars a year would be the opportunity cost of buying the machinery for your tire factory.

John and Carla each earn $50,000 a year. Their family income is $100,000. They decide to have a baby, and Carla chooses to stay at home for five years to raise the child. The opportunity cost of that decision, staying at home and not working, is $250,000.

An economist always considers opportunity costs. For everything you decide to do, there is something you miss out on.

If you want to save money by painting your house yourself, you save money, but the hours you put into it are the opportunity costs. Would your life have been better if you were free to use that time doing something other than painting?

President Eisenhower famously warned about the influences of the military-industrial complex. He pointed out that the money spent on a jet bomber equaled five high schools not being built or two hospitals not being constructed. Those five high schools not built are the opportunity costs for building that bomber. So governments too have opportunity costs.

3

THE INVISIBLE HAND

The author was taking a tour in Poland recently, and remarked to the tour guide about the great improvement in the Polish economy since the fall of communism. When asked how the great economic turned around had happened, the guide smiled and responded "the invisible hand."

The phrase "the invisible hand" is a popular and important economic term. Yet many people are not sure what it means. It may be a bit of an over simplification to state that "the invisible hand" means supply and demand. A more in depth understanding of the phrase would be as follows: *People will almost always act in their own self-interests. This is not a bad thing because when people are free to do this this, a nation, and a society as a whole benefits.*

Adam Smith coined this term in 1776 in his seminal work *The Wealth of Nations.* As popular as this phrase is today, it should be pointed out that Smith used the term only three times. Smith famously wrote:" *By pursuing his own interest he frequently promotes that of the society more effectually than when he really intends to promote it. I have never known much good done by those who affected to trade for the public good.*"

Smith further stated: "*by directing his industry in such a manner as its produce may be of the greatest value, he intends only his own gain, and he is in this, as in many other cases, led by an invisible hand to promote an end which was no part of his intention.*

What Smith is saying is this: *if we are acting in our own self-interest, all of us together, whether we know it or not, we are helping society as a whole.*

It would be fair to say, that if Smith were alive today, he would probably be a Republican.

In contemporary times, some equate Smiths invisible hand idea as justifying greed. Smith never condoned greed, and saw a big difference between acting in ones self interest and greed. Smith also did not view all regulation as being bad. The concept of the invisible hand can often be taken too far by its adherents.

4

CAPITALISM

—᙭—

Capitalism is such an important component of the American DNA that it is generally considered unpatriotic to question it or criticize it. Even accomplished economists are hesitant to be viewed as apostates.

Capitalism, as an economic system, has a rather simple definition. It refers to an economic system where capital (the buildings, machinery, companies, and the like) that are used to produce services or goods are owned by private individuals, not the government. It also can mean, somewhat confusingly, that it is the public that owns companies, by buying shares in them or loaning money to them for bonds. (Certainly, it can also be said that the public owns the local municipal sewage treatment plant that tax dollars pay to build and operate. This is where things get a tad confusing).

Capitalism is a lot more complicated than described above. So complicated, in fact, that many economists are hesitant to define it. Capitalism is really an amalgamation of many systems, borrowing ideas from many divergent economic theories.

One thing is certain, however. Capitalism and "free market" are often terms used somewhat interchangeably. Why? Because it is the people, not the state, that dominate the direction of the economy.

Capitalists that are "true believers" generally eschew government regulation.

It must be pointed out that there is really no such thing as a totally capitalist economy in the developed world today. All "capitalist" countries do have significant governmental regulations, government intervention in the economy, and even government owned (or mostly government owned) industries. Therefore, most countries with a capitalist economic system are more accurately described as being "mixed economies".

A pharmaceutical firm may not have the money to develop a cure for a rare disease. The government may have to provide the money, or incentive for a company to do so, especially when the outlook for a newly developed drug suggests there is little or no profit to be made.

This would be an example of government intervention in a "mixed economy". An action that is decidedly uncapitalistic.

In reality, economic systems that are totally capitalistic (or laissez-faire economies, from the French for "let them do it as they wish") have never really existed. All existing capitalist economies are really mixed economies.

Capitalism had its origins in feudalism, where peasants sold their labor to the landed gentry. Feudalism gave way to mercantilism, which provided an emphasis on trade between nations as a means of enrichment.

Capitalism and democracy are very compatible, that "invisible hand" described earlier, is inherently democratic. If the invisible hand is democratic in nature, should not the same be said about labor unions?

Winston Churchill once said "the inherent vice of capitalism is the unequal sharing of blessings: the inherent virtue of socialism is the equal sharing of miseries"

Michael Moore stated: "Capitalism is an organized system to guarantee that greed becomes the primary force of our economic system and allows the few at the top to get very wealthy and has the rest of us riding around thinking we can be that way, too - if we just work hard enough, sell enough Tupperware and Amway products, we can get a pink Cadillac."

John Maynard Keynes said:
"Capitalism is the astounding belief that the most wickedest of men will do the most wickedest of things for the greatest good of everyone."

Finally, it is said by Ayaan Hirsi Ali that "Liberal capitalism is not perfect, but compared to the other 'isms,' it's far superior.

5

SUPPLY-SIDE ECONOMICS

Supply-side economics is a school of thought of macroeconomics (we shall soon discuss macroeconomics at length) that argues that economic growth can be effectively encouraged by lowering barriers for people to produce (supply) goods and services as well as lowering barriers for people investing in capital. Supply-side economics suggests consumers will then benefit from a greater supply of goods and services at lower prices and that the investment and expansion of businesses will increase the demand for employees. Typical policy recommendations of supply-side economists are lower tax rates and less regulation of businesses.

The Laffer curve is a major tenet of supply side economics: it suggests that government tax revenues from a specific tax are the same (nil) at 100% tax rates as at 0% tax rates respectively. The tax rate that achieves optimum, or highest government revenues is somewhere in between these two values.

As in classical economics, supply-side economics proposed that production or supply is the key to economic prosperity and that consumption or demand is merely a secondary consequence. Early this idea had been summarized in Say's Law of economics, which states: "A product is no sooner created, than it, from that instant, affords a market for other products to the full extent of its own value." John Maynard Keynes, the founder of Keynesianism, summarized Say's Law as "supply creates its own demand." He turned Say's Law on its head in the 1930s by declaring that demand creates its own supply.

In 1978, Jude Wanniski published *The Way the World Works*, in which he laid out the central thesis of supply-side economics and detailed the failure of high tax-rate progressive income tax systems and U.S. monetary policy under Nixon in the 1970s. Wanniski advocated lower tax rates and a return to some kind of gold standard, similar to the 1944–1971 Bretton Woods System that Nixon abandoned.

In 1983, economist Victor Canto, a disciple of Arthur Laffer, published *The Foundations of Supply-Side Economics*. This theory focuses on the effects of marginal tax rates on the incentive to work and save, which affect the growth of the "supply side" or what Keynesians call potential output. While the latter focus on changes in the rate of supply-side growth in the long run, the "new" supply-siders often promised short-term results.

Most recently, supply-side advocates push hard for low taxes and tax cuts. The more people have to pay in taxes, they argue, the greater will be their incentive to avoid paying them or to work (produce) less.

6

KEYNESIAN ECONOMICS

—ᴡᴡ—

The core belief of Keynesian economists is that government spending and taxation can and should be used to manage, direct, or even control the economy. Want to encourage solar energy? Give tax credits to people that install solar panels on the roofs of their homes. Want to increase the percentage of people that own homes? Let them deduct from their income taxes what they spend for interest on their mortgages.

John Maynard Keynes, a British economist-philosopher developed this theory among others in his 1936 work *The General Theory of Employment, Interest, and Money*. This book was written of course during the Great Depression. Keynes posited that government has a duty to help the economy during troubled times, hence the great spending programs by governments during the Great Depression to employ people. The American President FDR was certainly a Keynesian, as was President Obama during the recent financial calamity.

Keynesian economists advocate that the government borrow money during hard times to build infrastructure for the common good, hire public employees and contractors to build these improvements to pump money into the moribund economy. It is often suggested that interest rates be lowered during bad times in an effort to encourage private companies to borrow so they can expand, spend more, and employ more people.

If a local government builds a new hospital during hard times, many construction workers get hired, paid, and spend their salaries helping all manner of local businesses.

There are half dozen principles of Keynesian economics:

- The short-term is important. Short-term unemployment can cause long-term problems.
- Economies can be unpredictable, and are influenced by both private and public spending and decisions.
- It is the government's responsibility to attempt to keep unemployment percentages down and not leave that to "the indivisible hand."
- Salaries and prices are impacted by supply and demand, but move slowly nonetheless.
- Economies do have "boom" and "bust" cycles, but that does not mean that government policy should not try to smooth them out and make them less painful.
- Philosophically, Keynesians though concerned about inflation, tend to be more concerned about unemployment.

It may be fair to say that even the most ardent of opponents to Keynesian theory, become Keynesian's when times become extremely rough and dangerous.

7

MONETARISM

—ɯ—

Monetarism is an economic theory that competes with, and is much different from, Keynesian theory. Monetarism is associated with another giant in the field of economics Milton Friedman. Dr. Friedman put forth his theory of monetarism in his seminal book *A Monetary History of the United States* in 1971. Friedman won the Nobel Prize for economics in 1976.

Friedman suggests that inflation is a much more serious ill than unemployment. He felt that when governments pump money into the economy (a Keynesian approach) that inflation increases and causes great harm to the economy. His theory suggests that if central banks were tasked with controlling prices, other parts of the economy (such as unemployment and productivity) would take care of themselves.

Monetarists assert that workers should be encouraged to accept lower wages, and will view doing so desirable to increased inflation. Friedman and his followers also believe in controlling the money supply: print too much money and inflation ensues.

Monetarists also believe that independent central banks should control the economy by adjusting interest rates as needed, as opposed to the Keynesian's who see more of a role for politicians in the economy.

Ronald Reagan of the US and Margaret Thatcher of the UK were prominent monetarists.

Monetarism and Keynesianism remain popular and competing economic philosophies to this day. It is said that many Democrats are Keynesians and many Republicans are Monetarists.

8

MONEY

There have been some interesting things said about money:

When I was young I thought that money was the most important thing in life; now that I am old I know that it is.
Oscar Wilde
Money has never made man happy, nor will it; there is nothing in its nature to produce happiness. The more of it one has the more one wants.
Benjamin Franklin
A little thought and a little kindness are often worth more than a great deal of money.
John Ruskin
The lack of money is the root of all evil.
Mark Twain
Money cannot buy peace of mind. It cannot heal ruptured relationships, or build meaning into a life that has none.
Richard M. DeVos
Wealth is the ability to fully experience life.
Henry David Thoreau

Economists recognize two categories of money:

1. Fiat money-money without intrinsic value. A government has simply stated that that particular unit of money has a certain legal value.
2. Commodity money- money that has intrinsic value, such as a gold coin. Gold is a valuable metal.

Economists measure money in the following ways:

M1- the amount of money in circulation in the country outside of banks, and in bank accounts that people can access. In other words, the amount of money people can get their hands on and spend.

M2-money that is less liquid, that may take some time for people to access, such as money in a certificate of deposit that has not yet matured. (Along with the money in the M1 category).
M3-Close equivalents of money, like money market funds and other investments (along with M1 and M2).

The central banks use these measures to account for how much money is available in our society.

The basis of money is trust. Is it worth what the government says it is worth? After all, a mere piece of paper has a real intrinsic value of almost nothing. Because trust is so important in money having real value, governments must do all they can to keep their word, and honor the value of the money.

Money is a medium of exchange that makes complex modern societies possible. It is also something resistant to loosing value. Money functions as something that allows credit to be possible. This is very important to a societies growth, security, and productivity.

9

MICROECONOMICS VS MACROECONOMICS

—m—

Microeconomics refers to the study of individuals and business decisions, whereas macroeconomics focus higher up at the level of country and governmental economic decisions.

Macroeconomics and microeconomics, and their range of underlying concepts, have been the subject of a great deal of study. These fields of study are vast; here is a brief summary of what each covers:

Microeconomics is the study of decisions that people and businesses make regarding the allocation of resources and the prices of goods and services. This means taking into account taxes and regulations created by a nations governments. Microeconomics focuses on supply and demand and other forces that determine price levels seen in the economy. For example, microeconomics would look at how a specific company could maximize it's production and capacity so it could lower prices and better compete in its industry.

Macroeconomics, however, is the field of economics that studies the behavior of the economy as whole, not just specific companies, but entire industries and economies. "Macro" looks at economy-wide phenomena, such as Gross National Product (GNP) and how it is affected by changes in unemployment, national income, rate of growth, and price levels. Macroeconomics would address how an increase/decrease in net exports would affect a nation's capital account or how GNP would be affected by the unemployment rate.

While these two studies of economics appear to be different, they are actually interdependent and complement one another since there are many overlapping issues between the two fields. For example, increased inflation (a macro effect) would cause the price of raw materials to increase for companies and in turn affect the end product's price charged to the public.

To put it simply, microeconomics takes a bottoms-up approach to analyzing the economy while macroeconomics takes a top-down approach. Regardless, both micro- and macroeconomics provide fundamental tools for any finance professional, business owner, or lawmaker and should be studied together in order to fully understand how companies operate and earn revenues and thus, how an entire economy is managed and sustained.

10

CENTRAL BANKING AND INTEREST RATES

—⚯—

It is the prime responsibility of the central banker, the person in charge of a nation's monetary policy (it's interest rates), to make sure that the countries economy does not overheat or sink into a depression. In short, to keep the economy at an even keel. How does one do this?

When an economy is going full boar, and great profits are to be had, there is a danger that inflation will ensue, and that this will be harmful to the populace. High inflation can hurt. A central banker has to dampen the party. How is this done? -By raising interest rates. Business slows down when it costs more for businesses to borrow. If the economy slows down, often inflation does as well.

The reverse is true when an economy is weak. If interest rates are lowered, business borrowing increases, more products and services are produced, and an economy heats up.

Central banks in advanced economies are generally independent of governmental authority so it is easier for them to do the right thing, and not be influenced by politics or politicians.

Central bankers are only as good, in some respects, as the statistics they base their decisions on.

11

INFLATION

Inflation refers to the rising prices of goods and services. Hopefully, it is slow and predictable. Making sure that is both slow and predictable is one of the major functions of a nation's central bank.

Inflation is usually talked about in terms of one year. Hence, a five percent inflation rate means that prices have risen five percent in the last twelve months. Inflation gives us a sense of the health of an economy.

How is inflation measured? In four ways:

1. The Consumer Price Index: the price of a standard "basket" of goods and services is monitored monthly.
2. The Retail Price Index: this is a bit more comprehensive and is used in Great Britain. It includes such things as home ownership costs and the like.
3. The Product Price Index: This involves recording the cost of raw materials for manufacturers, and the prices they charge retailers for selling the final product.
4. Gross Domestic Product Deflator: This is the most comprehensive of all measures as it measures costs of all goods across a nation. Because it is so comprehensive, it is computed less frequently.

Measuring inflation is important because it tells us a lot about the condition of a society. Are wages keeping up with the cost of living? If not, people will be hurting. Their standard of living is declining. Ones standard of living can decline even if their income increases if their income increases less than the rise of prices they must pay for goods and services.

When an economy is strong and growing people will receive raises and spend more money. This causes more demand, and thus higher prices for goods and services, or inflation. When an economy is less healthy, spending goes down, thus demand goes down, and theoretically prices should go down as well.

The prices of goods are impacted both by demand and how much money people have to spend.

Is it important to have inflation as a permanent phenomenon? Probably. Here is why our leaders want some inflation (but not too much):

1. Inflation makes it likely that people will spend and not just save their money. If prices are going up, you want to buy that refrigerator before it gets too expensive. When you do buy it, the manufacturer of that fridge, the store that sold it to you, and others benefit. The economy develops some momentum, which is important.
2. People are used to and expect higher wages. When that does not happen, they feel they are spinning their wheels.

Too much inflation is bad. It hurts a person's standard of living. Too little inflation is also an undesirable thing. Inflation is best in the "goldilocks" zone. Just the right amount.

Central Banks try to keep inflation steady, predictable, and gradual.

12

UNEMPLOYMENT

Economics certainly has some central issues: interest rates, gross domestic product, inflation, and the like. No area of economic study is more important than the unemployment rate. Full employment, or significantly reduced unemployment rates are part and parcel of every political campaign.

Government is always keen on reducing the unemployment rate because of the significant misery involved in unemployment for the people involved. Companies, however, require a large degree of freedom to make an economy dynamic. Therefore, the government and the private sector may not always see eye to eye on the importance of keeping the unemployment rate down.

In some parts of the developed world, Europe, for example, there are many legal safeguards restricting an employer's ability to fire workers, or restrict their hours or benefits. But in the United States economic philosophies are somewhat different. In the US the guiding philosophy seems to be that job security measures may save jobs for current workers but reduce flexibility and efficiency in the overall economy, thus hurting growth and future job creation. Whatever side of this philosophical argument you come down on, it should be noted that new jobs are created at a higher rate in the United States where the labor market is more flexible.

Unemployment can be defined simplistically. One does not have a job. Things are not always so cut and dried though, especially to economists. How do you classify someone that has a temporary job they are over qualified for? How do you classify someone who lost his or her job in an industry that is now obsolete? Is that person different from someone that just lost their job and they have skills and training that are in demand?

Most economists throughout the world define unemployment as not having a job and actively looking for work. Such a definition would not include people deciding to not work to care for a child, or making the choice of taking time off because their spouse is well paid. It is important to consider the age of an unemployed person when studying unemployment numbers. Younger people that are unemployed for long periods of time find it very difficult to get back into the workforce.

Inflation and unemployment are closely related. When unemployment is low, employers must offer higher wages to attract workers. This of course requires prices for goods and services to increase, thus increasing inflation. The reverse is also true. When unemployment is high, workers are willing to take any job, at lower rates of pay, just to have a job. This lowers wages, which lowers the costs of goods and services, and thus decreases inflation.

Though full employment is always a stated goal of politicians, economists believe it is not really attainable, or perhaps even desirable in a free economy.

Sometimes unemployment pays. And government unwittingly encourages unemployment. The great comedian Bob Newhart tells the story of working forty hours a week for the government passing out unemployment checks of $78 a week to unemployed people. For this he was paid $80 a week. How long did it take Bob to want to be fired?

13

TAXES

"In this world nothing can be said to be certain except death and taxes." Everyone knows this quote, but few know whom to attribute it to. None other than Benjamin Franklin, the Yogi Berra of his time, first said it. His quote is true enough, but if he were alive today he would probably have said "In this world nothing can be said to be certain except death and taxes and the Chicago Cubs not playing baseball in October."

Taxes have been, and will probably always be, one of the most bitterly fought over subjects in politics. No one likes to pay them, and everyone wants the services they pay for.

Taxes have always been linked to the desire of people to have a say as to how their money is spent. So, in essence, taxes promote democracy. They also promote revolution, as evidenced by the Boston Tea party.

In modern times, taxes have increased as governments world wide have increased their efforts to improve education, welfare, security for the elderly, healthcare, and the like. Increasingly, these services are considered rights by citizens.

There are all manner of taxes governments levy to raise funds for these services: income taxes, sales taxes, property taxes, inheritance taxes, capital gains taxes, wealth taxes, and the like. "Sin" taxes (taxes on alcohol and tobacco, for example) not only raise funds for government, but also discourage behavior that is not always in a person's best interest. This brings us to an often forgotten function of taxes: they discourage some behaviors; just as tax breaks encourage some behaviors (for example tax write offs for mortgage interest promote home ownership)

Many different levels of government assess taxes. There are federal taxes, state taxes, county taxes, municipal taxes, and even local taxing bodies such as school districts, library districts, mosquito abatement districts, and the like.

In his treaties The Wealth of Nations, Adam Smith laid out some guidelines for taxation that are largely honored today:

1. Tax should be certain, not arbitrary, with collection times uniform and transparent.
2. Citizens should contribute in proportion to their income.
3. Taxes should be no more than necessary (both to the citizenry and their government).
4. Tax should come due at a logical time. (When you purchase an item that is when you pay the sales tax.)

Generally, when taxes go up, people try harder to evade them, thus increasing the "off the books" economy.

Once a tax is instituted, historically, it seldom goes away.

There are many things that should be thought of as a type of taxation, that often are not. State Lotteries, for example. They raise money for the state from the people. These types of taxes tend to be paid more by the less affluent, then the affluent, and thus are said to be regressive. Often, the less affluent participate in the lottery, in hopes that they can become members of the affluent class.

14

DEFLATION AND DEBT-SUDDENLY RELEVANT

—〰—

Deflation happens when prices fall (the opposite of inflation). When prices fall the money you earn, the money you have saved, is worth more. In many ways, this is a good thing. In some ways it is not. In the past, deflation was universally viewed as a positive thing. Now, economists find aspects of it somewhat worrisome.

Significant deflation became problematic during our Great Depression. Prices went down dramatically. Wages also decreased dramatically. Values of homes decreased significantly. But ones debt remained the same. People had less money to pay off their debts, and a crisis ensued.

When prices go down, people tend to hang on to their money. Their money is now more valuable, and getting more so as time goes on. Less money being spent means less products and services purchased. Fewer things bought hurts employment numbers and/or wages. So deflation is not necessarily a good thing.

Sometimes technology can reduce the price of goods. Money buys more, becomes more valuable as a result, and deflation ensues. Technology might also reduce the number of people that have jobs, or at least higher paying jobs. The bottom line: deflation can be a mixed blessing. (Not that high inflation should be viewed as a good thing).

Psychologically, people like to see their numbers go up. They like their salary to increase each year, the value of their home to increase each year. Deflation then, psychologically, can be stressful. Some of us perceive that we are spinning our wheels.

In some cases deflation can hurt businesses. They are forced to lower prices to retain market share and compete, as prices are going down in their market, but they are contractually obligated to wages by contract that cannot go down. This may require them to lay off workers, as they cannot lower their wages.

Deflation happens when the amount of money in an economic system falls, or the supply of goods and services increases.

(Inflation happens when too much money chases too few goods. Deflation is the exact opposite).

Central banks can deal with inflation by increasing interest rates. Deflation is not so easy to deal with; they cannot lower interest rates to below zero. What central banks can do to address deflation is called quantitative easing. This means they increase the amount of cash in circulation, they can do this by a variety of means: increasing the amount of money commercial banks have in their vaults, buying assets such as bonds, etc.

15

THE IMPORTANCE OF ENERGY AND PETROCHEMICALS

—ɯɯ—

Commodities are important. Grains, raw materials used for building and manufacturing, potable water; all manner of commodities are important economically. Perhaps none more so than oil. Few commodities are as problematic as oil, though access to clean water will soon become as troublesome.

When oil prices rise, the cost of living goes up. It costs more to manufacture goods, power homes and cars, and generate electricity. Everyone and everything is impacted by higher oil prices. Rising oil prices impact people every bit as much as rising taxes. When oil prices go up, no one is immune. Everyone has less disposable income, because they are paying more to commute, more to power their home, and more for goods that have increased in price due to the rising energy costs.

It should be pointed out that oil is not required only for energy production. It is an essential component in fertilizer, and necessary to the manufacture of plastics.

Oil is so important to a nations economy, that access to it, and the price of this commodity, is viewed as an essential part of a nations' security. Without access to oil, and oil at an affordable price, a nations' national security is severely weakened.

Increased oil prices can lead to inflation. Dramatically increased oil prices can result in ruinous inflation. Such oil induced shock occurred in the United States 1973-1975. Ever since this time, the United States has viewed the goal of energy independence as being a matter of national security.

Terrorism in the parts of the world that produce the oil we need to import impacts our national security. If terrorists shut down production, our oil supply decreases and/or becomes more expensive. This is one reason our military expenditures are high. We need to be ready to protect our oil sources. It is also a reason we continue to seek energy independence through any means, including alternative energy sources.

16

GLOBALIZATION

—⁓—

Today. Over morning coffee, you can pick up your laptop and order an item manufactured anywhere on the planet and have it delivered to your home in days. Globalization is a fact of life, and has certainly existed since, and even before, the voyage of Christopher Columbus, a voyage that eventuated a significant uptick in world trade. Like anything else, globalization has its good points and bad points.

There are six components to globalization to be understood:

1. Unstoppable- it is here to stay. A fact of life. We cannot ignore it or wish it away.
2. Outsourcing-corporations will shift their production of goods and services to locations where they can be produced more cheaply (usually due to cheaper labor availability). Factory workers in China and Vietnam make less per hour than factory workers in the United States. An Indian radiologist can read a digital x-ray and interpret it for a smaller fee than an American radiologist.
3. Liberalization-nations are opening themselves up to foreign corporations and foreign workers, in part, because they want their companies welcome in foreign markets.
4. Legal consistency-nations are improving rule of law, especially in business, and protecting intellectual property rights, so that foreigners will set up shop comfortably in their nation. They want the world community to feel safe doing business in their country.
5. Free trade-Tariffs and other barriers to trade are lessened or coming down. Foreign investment is encouraged. This has its good points and bad points. Lowering trade barriers may lead to the death of a domestic industry. It also can lead to other nations allowing in goods and services produced by your country.
6. Communication-the Internet allows workers all over the world to collaborate on projects in real time. This is truly the global age of research and development.

The more intertwined nations become due to globalization, the more dependent they are on one another, the less likely it is that they will see benefit from going to war with each other. Also, it seems more likely that culture itself may become more uniform and less country specific.

17

TECHNOLOGICAL ADVANCES

—◆—

The easiest way to consider the importance of technological advancement to the field of economics is to conceptualize that advancement as having occurred in three stages (so far).

1. The first industrial revolution-
    This happened between the mid-1700's and the early 1800's and was marked by the invention of the steam engine. The steam engine allowed human productivity to multiply at astounding rates. Industrial activity was no longer reliant on wind or water-power. Coal could now be used. (Centuries later we realized that this is a double-edged sword in terms of our environment). The first industrial revolution led to increased wealth, increased family size, and increased hope.

2. The second industrial revolution-
    The second industrial revolution involves the use and proliferation of electricity, oil, and metallurgy (creating steel and the like for the building of infrastructure and industry). Automobiles, aviation, and transportation allowed for great improvements in transporting people, goods, and services. Nations that improved in these areas became globally prominent and powerful.

3. The third industrial revolution-
    The third revolution involves the creation of computers and the advent of the Internet. This has led to great increases in productivity and hastened the speed of globalization.

One might reasonably argue we are now in a fourth revolution. The revolution of biology. Now that we have solved the human genome, advances in medicine, and indeed, changes in the human species, will occur at an unforeseen and rapid pace.

18

CREATIVE DESTRUCTION

Here we are, about to discuss one of the more painful and controversial ideas of economics: creative destruction.

According to the Austrian economist Joseph Schumpeter, Creative destruction describes the "process of industrial mutation that incessantly revolutionizes the economic structure from within, incessantly destroying the old one, incessantly creating a new one.

Creative destruction can cause temporary economic distress, such as layoffs of workers with obsolete working skills and loss of income or return on investment on the parts of business owners, financiers, and investors. With regard to the workers, though a continually innovating economy generates new opportunities to participate in more creative and productive enterprises (provided they can acquire the necessary skills), creative destruction can cause severe hardship in the short term.

In simple terms, old industries die off when technology or methods improve. Often, many of their workers must adapt to that change. Not all do, and some loose their jobs. Their families suffer. The onward advancement of the economy continues, but there are casualties in that advancement. Some of us become obsolete when there is progress. If you are one of those that become obsolete, was the progress, the overall good worth it?

19

GOVERNMENTAL DEFICITS

—m—

A government is said to be running a deficit when it spends more money in a year than it takes in from taxes and other fees. When this happens it is called a budget deficit or a fiscal deficit. As you know, families cannot run this way long, but governments can. Governments can always print more money, families cannot (unless they want to get in a whole lot of trouble and spend some time in the old "gray bar hotel").

Sometimes it makes sense for a family to run a deficit. Borrowing money for a child's eduction is a good example of a temporary deficit that will yield long-term benefits. Sometimes, a family may have housing or medical issues that need to be addressed. There is certainly a concept of good debt and bad debt. The same is true for government. Borrowing money for infrastructure: building roads and bridges that will increase an areas economic output in the long term, may often be a good example of spending outpacing revenue being a good thing.

How does a government spend most of its money? Someone once said a government is like an insurance company with an army. In our country most governmental money is spent on "mandatory" things such as social security, medicaid, and defense.

State governments also tax and spend, as do city and county governments. As these entities cannot print money as the federal government can, they cannot run deficits as long.

When countries borrow too much because they are taking in less money than they spend there are some negative consequences:

1. The value of the nation's currency weakens.
2. People and businesses from other nations are less likely to invest there.
3. Future generations are saddled with the debt.

Most modern nations run at a deficit. The key is knowing the difference between good debt and bad debt. The same is true for a typical family.

20

RISING INEQUALITY

The combined wealth of the world's 85 richest people ($1.7 trillion) is now equivalent to that held by the poorest half of the planet's population, or 3.5 billion people.

The ratio of CEO pay to average worker pay is now as follows:
United States 354:1
Switzerland 148:1
Germany 147:1
Spain 127:1

The above trends appear, by all accounts, to be accelerating.

What implications does this rising inequality have for our future?

Nations, especially wealthy ones, tend to tax the ultra-rich to provide benefits for the very poor. This is especially true in the Nordic nations. This approach to dealing with inequality is often referred to as "the Swedish" model.

As workers come to realize that the mega-rich have accumulated their wealth in many cases from the labor of people much less wealthy, will capitalism itself be in jeopardy?

21

PROTECTIONISM

—⟋⟍—

Protectionism is a governmental policy of protecting domestic industries against foreign competition by means of tariffs, subsidies, import quotas, or other restrictions or barriers placed on the imports of foreign competitors goods and services. Protectionist policies have been implemented by most countries, despite the fact that most economists agree that the world economy generally benefits overall from free trade.

Government-levied tariffs are among the chief protectionist measures. They raise the price of targeted imported articles, making them more expensive (and therefore less attractive to consumers) than domestic products. Protective tariffs have historically been employed to stimulate industries in countries beset by recession or depression. Protectionism may be helpful to new or developing industries in developing nations. It can also serve as a means of fostering self-sufficiency in defense industries or food production, two things important to national security. Import quotas offer another means of protectionism. These quotas set an absolute limit on the amount of certain goods that can be imported into a country and tend to be more effective than protective tariffs, which do not always dissuade consumers who are willing to pay a higher price for imported goods.

Protectionist policies by one nation often encourage retaliatory protectionist policies in the other nations they trade with.

Politicians are often pressured into protectionist policies, and implement them, even when they may not serve the long-term interests of their country.

22

ENVIRONMENTAL ECONOMICS

—◆—

Economics and the environment are closely related, and cannot be separated. The quest for economic development occurred by impacting the environment, usually, in negative ways. Countries have made great economic gains by exploiting their natural resources, and, in many cases, abusing their environment. Economics may be part of the remediation of our environment. Tax breaks for environmentally friendly methodology will help. Tax incentives for clean up may also be part of the solution. Economics then may become both the cause of, and solution for, environmental issues

We cannot escape the fact that strong lobbying forces hold sway over governmental policy. Powerful industries employ powerful lobbyists. They make huge campaign contributions to lawmakers charged with the responsibility of making laws that can protect our environment. Often, because of the support law makers receive from industry, they produce laws that protect industry, not the environment.

Economic development has costs. Pollution of the air and water allow for jobs in industry and profits. It also kills people from fouled air and water resources. Yet the costs of a product do not reflect the health costs many people incur.

Studies show that the costs of climate change could very well account for twenty percent of global gross domestic product. These same studies show that dealing with these issues may cost only one percent of global gross domestic product. Lawmakers have it within their power to pass laws requiring industry to spend this money. When legislators receive so much money in contributions from the industries they are supposed to oversee, it is difficult for them to pass laws that are in the best interests of the people and future generations.

The concept of externalities is important to understanding the relationship between the environment and economics.

Externality refers to a consequence of an economic activity that is experienced by unrelated third parties. An externality can be either positive or negative.

Pollution emitted by a factory that spoils the surrounding environment and affects the health of nearby residents is an example of a negative externality. An example of a positive externality is the effect of a well-educated labor force on the productivity of a company.

Economic activity must be viewed with all externalities considered. This approach will assist us in dealing with environmental issues before they become problematic.

What are some things that can be done, economically, that can help? In the area of emissions, there are four major adjustments that can make a huge difference:

1. Carbon trading- governments can auction or sell permits to industry to emit specified amounts of carbon. This will provide an incentive for industry to lessen its carbon footprint as they pay up front for some of the aforementioned externalities.
2. Technological improvements-green technologies that are less polluting can receive favorable tax treatment.
3. "Green taxes"- taxes on actions that increase pollution, for example, burning fossil fuels, will lead to cars that have much better gas mileage, electric car development, and the like.
4. Lawmakers need to have the courage to accept the science on climate change.

23

GAME THEORY

Game theory is a model of optimality taking into consideration not only benefits less costs, but also the interaction between participants.

Game theory looks at the relationships between participants in a particular model and predicts their optimal decisions.

What economists call game theory psychologists often call the theory of social situations, which is an accurate description of what game theory is all about. Game theory is relevant to parlor games such as poker or bridge, and most research in game theory focuses on how groups of people interact. There are two main branches of game theory: cooperative and noncooperative game theory. Noncooperative game theory deals largely with how intelligent individuals interact with one another in an effort to achieve their own goals.

In addition to game theory, economic theory has three other main branches: decision theory, general equilibrium theory and mechanism design theory. All are closely connected to game theory.

Decision theory can be viewed as a theory of one-person games, or a game of a single player against nature. The focus is on preferences and the formation of beliefs. The most widely used form of decision theory argues that preferences among risky alternatives can be described by the maximization of the expected value of a numerical utility function, where utility may depend on a number of things, but in situations of interest to economists often depends on money income. Probability theory is heavily used in order to represent the uncertainty of outcomes, and Bayes Law is frequently used to model the way in which new information is used to revise beliefs. Decision theory is often used in the form of decision analysis, which shows how best to acquire information before making a decision.

General equilibrium theory can be viewed as a specialized branch of game theory that deals with trade and production, and typically with a relatively large number of individual consumers and producers. It is widely used in the macroeconomic analysis of broad based economic policies such as monetary or tax policy, in finance to analyze stock markets, to study interest and exchange rates and other prices. In recent years, political economy has emerged as a combination of general equilibrium theory and game theory in which the private sector of the economy is modeled by general equilibrium theory, while voting behavior and the incentive of governments is analyzed using game theory. Issues studied include tax policy, trade policy, and the role of international trade agreements such as the European Union.

Mechanism design theory differs from game theory in that game theory takes the rules of the game as given, while mechanism design theory asks about the consequences of different types of rules. Naturally this relies heavily on game theory. Questions addressed by mechanism design theory include the design of compensation and wage agreements that effectively spread risk while maintaining incentives, and the design of auctions to maximize revenue, or achieve other goals.

The use of game theory in understanding the economy on both the macro and micro level is not only in vogue, but becoming increasingly important.

24

BEHAVIORAL ECONOMICS

Behavioral economics, as a school of thought, recognizes that people often do not make rational decisions. Often, they make decisions based on emotions. Hence the success of buy one get one free sales and the popularity of luxury brands.

Behavioral economists study why people behave irrationally. It is an area of economics that overlaps with psychology and marketing and is quite in vogue at present.

Behavioral economics has five basic principles:

1. People are not rational investors. They place more emphasis on the current situation as opposed to thinking long-term. (Hence, many of us are not prepared for retirement).
2. We often tend to follow the crowd. We make financial decisions based on what others do, rather than performing research.
3. People often invest in a way that they feel is ethically or morally right, not thinking in terms of what investment may make them the most money.
4. We often make decisions out of habit, and ignore new evidence. Old habits are hard to break.
5. People look at decisions involving money emotionally. Seeing a difference between a $20 cash gift and a $20 box of chocolates as a gift.

People make economic decisions based on emotions. Most agree that the government should protect people from dangerous products. But should the government "nudge" people into making financial decisions that are in their best interests? Such are the debates of the behavioral economists.

25

PENSIONS AND THE SOCIAL SAFETY NET

Most wealthy countries subscribe to the following philosophy:

People should contribute money through taxes when they are working and in good health so that they can receive benefits when they are ill and unable to work or old and seek to retire.

Pensions actually got a great boost from the American Civil War. Due to the high death rate, enlistments were down. Pensions for veterans enticed many to enlist. In Europe, Otto Von Bismarck established pensions and health insurance in 1880. In 1908, David Lloyd George initiated pensions in the United Kingdom.

Pensions are recognized by most economists as a transfer of wealth to the old from the young in that people, due to greater life expectancy, often seem to obtain more from their pension than they pay into it when they are younger. It is thought that this is something we owe people for a lifetime of work and building the country. There are worries, however, that it can be unsustainable.

There are some things that can be considered to make pensions and the social safety net sustainable:

1. All people should be required to make monthly contributions (probably at a higher rate than they are now) while they are working.
2. Allow more immigrants. They can pay taxes to the general fund to support the health and retirement of older people and ill people, and maybe even return to their home countries and not draw benefits, or at least some of their benefits.
3. Raise taxes to pay for the social safety net (at the risk of slowed economic growth).

4. Require people to work longer, receive less benefits in retirement, or "means test" retirement benefits. (A multi-millionaire, despite having contributed money to the government over his or her working life may receive less or no benefits when they retire).

26

BUSTS AND BOOMS

—ɯɯ—

There are always busts and booms in the economy and probably always will be.

The "bust and boom cycle" can be defined as a process of economic expansion and contraction that occurs repeatedly. The boom and bust cycle is a key characteristic of modern capitalist economies. During a boom the economy grows, jobs are in good supply and the market brings higher returns to investors. In the subsequent bust the economy shrinks, people lose their jobs and investors lose money. Boom-bust cycles last for varying lengths of time; they also vary in severity.

Since the end of World War II, the US has experienced twelve boom-bust cycles. Why do we have a boom and bust cycle instead of a long, steady economic growth period? Because of the way central banks handle the money supply.

During a boom, the central bank makes it easier to obtain credit by lending money at low interest rates. Individuals and businesses can borrow money easily and cheaply and invest it in, say, technology equities or housing. People earn high returns on their investments, and the economy grows.

The problem is that when credit is very easy to obtain and interest rates are quite low, people will overinvest. This excess investment is called "malinvestment". There won't be enough demand for, say, all the homes that have been built, and the bust cycle will commence. Things that have been overinvested in will decline in value. Investors lose money, consumers cut spending and companies cut jobs. Credit becomes more difficult to obtain as boom-time borrowers become unable to make their loan repayments. The bust periods are referred to as recessions; if the recession is particularly severe, it is called a depression. Recently, we experienced what is now called "the great recession."

Government subsidies that make it less expensive to invest also contribute to the boom-bust cycle by encouraging companies and individuals to overinvest in the subsidized item. For example, the mortgage interest tax deduction subsidizes a home purchase by making the mortgage interest less expensive. The subsidy encourages more people to buy homes.

27

BANKS

A bank can be defined as a financial institution licensed as a receiver of deposits. There are two types of banks:

1. Commercial/retail banks
2. Investment banks.

Most nations have banks regulated by their governments.

Commercial banks are primarily concerned with managing withdrawals and deposits as well as supplying short-term loans to individuals and small businesses. Consumers use these banks for basic checking and savings accounts, certificates of deposit and sometimes for home mortgages.

Investment banks focus on providing services such as underwriting and corporate reorganization to institutional clients.

While many banks have both a physical brick-and-mortar and online presence, some banks have only an online presence. This is a relatively new innovation. Online-only banks often offer consumers higher interest rates and lower fees because they have fewer overheads. . Convenience, interest rates and fees are the driving factors in consumers' decisions of which bank to do business with. As an alternative to banks, consumers can opt to use a local credit union.

28

STOCKS

Stocks (often called equities) are a type of security that implies partial ownership in a corporation and represents a claim on part of the corporation's assets and earnings.

There are two main types of stock:

1. Common
2. Preferred

Common stock most often entitles the owner to vote at shareholders' meetings and to receive dividends.

Preferred stock often does not have voting rights, but has a higher claim on assets and earnings than the common shares. Owners of preferred stock receive dividends before common shareholders and have priority in the event that a company goes bankrupt and is liquidated.

A stockholder (or shareholder) has a claim to a part of the corporation's assets and earnings. In other words, a shareholder is an owner of a company. Ownership is determined by the number of shares a person owns in relation to the number of outstanding shares. For example, if a company has 100,000 shares of stock outstanding and one person owns 10,000 shares, that person would own and have claim to 10% of the company's assets.

Stocks are the foundation of nearly everyone's personal portfolio. Generally, they have outperformed most other investments over the long run.

The first such company recognized of this type was the Virginia Company, which was organized to finance trade between Britain and it's American colony. Next came the British East India Company, a monopoly granted by the crown, to facilitate trade between Britain and it's Asian possessions. Then came the Dutch East India Company, which performed a similar function for the Netherlands.

These corporations were different from their predecessors (guilds and partnerships) for the following reasons:

1. Limited liability-stock holders could only loose what they had invested in the company if it ran into problems.
2. Money raising-the companies offered shares to investors. These investors became owners of the company in proportion to the percentage of shares they owned.
3. Shareholders could sell their shares-shareholders could freely sell their sock, their percentage of ownership, to anyone else.

29

BONDS

—ɯ—

A bond is a "debt investment" in which an investor loans money to an entity (usually a corporation in needs of funds or a governmental body such as a school district or airport), which borrows the funds for a defined period of time at a variable or fixed interest rate. Companies, municipalities, states and even national governments raise money and finance a variety of projects and activities through the use of bonds. Owners of bonds are called debt holders, or creditors, of the issuer of these bonds.

Bonds are commonly referred to as fixed-income securities and are one of the three main generic asset classes, along with stocks (equities) and cash equivalents. Many corporate and government bonds are publicly traded on exchanges, while others are traded only over-the-counter (OTC).

When companies or other organizations must raise money to finance new projects, maintain ongoing operations, or refinance other existing debts, they may issue bonds directly to investors instead of obtaining loans from a bank. The indebted entity (issuer) issues a bond that contractually states the interest rate (coupon) that will be paid and the time at which the loaned funds (bond principal) must be returned (maturity date).

The issuance price of a bond is typically set at par, usually $100 or $1,000 face value per individual bond. The actual market price of a bond depends on a number of factors including the credit quality of the issuer, the length of time until expiration, and the coupon rate compared to the general interest rate environment at the time.

Bonds began in medieval Italy when its various city-states were at war. Their governments required the wealthy citizens to lend it money to fight these wars in exchange for interest payments on the amount borrowed. In modern times, citizens can finance government operations by voluntarily buying government bonds. This is often done by large pension funds.

30

THE FUTURE

New specialties in economics, especially behavioral economics, will receive increased attention. We now know many people do not make economic decisions rationally. They copy others or make decisions based on their own experiences, rather than doing real research and evaluation. It is very possible that this finding may lead governments to become more paternalistic in their regulation of the economy. For example, mortgage markets may become more regulated so that people are less apt to make decisions that are not in their long-term self-interest.

In the past, we trusted markets to regulate themselves. This has often been a miss-placed trust. Governments may become less dependent on the market to regulate the economy, and more likely to regulate the economy through rules and regulations.

Future economists will eclectically borrow from the following schools of thought: Keynesianism, behavioral economics, rational market theory, and monetarism.

BONUS SECTION
TWELVE IMPORTANT
ECONOMISTS IN HISTORY

—⁓—

Top economists in history:

John Locke – A pioneer in discussing the accumulation of private property in the mid 1600's.

David Ricardo – Important writer in the early 1800's on free trade (specialization and comparative advantage) and the rise of capitalism.

Irving Fisher – An American monetarist in the first half of the twentieth century, wrote 'The Debt-Deflation Theory of Great Depressions' in 1933, also wrote 'The Theory of Interest'

Joseph Schumpeter – Austrian economist specializing in business cycle theory, wrote 'Business Cycles' in 1939.

Friedrich A. Hayek – Member of the modern Austrian school, along with Ludwig von Mises, defenders of democracy and free-markets against socialist thought in the mid-twentieth century. Best books: The Road to Serfdom (Hayek, 1944) and Human Action (Mises, 1949). A very influential economist to this day.

Alan Greenspan – A pioneer in macro-economic modeling and forecasting, also a FED Chairman for almost two decades.

Milton Friedman –A modern day monetarist. A staunch defender of free markets and of limited government intervention.

Karl Marx –The father of socialist economics. He was very influential from mid-1800's to mid-1900's, but not as influential today.

John M. Keynes - Father of Keynesian economics. He introduced modern macroeconomics in both theory and policy to the world.

Adam Smith – Revolutionized economics by writing 'The Wealth of Nations' in 1776. He is still revered today as father of economics, political economist and moral philosopher. Smith posited that pursuit of individual self-interest acts as an "invisible hand" to contribute to the common good.

Robert Reich-Believes that "taxes are the price we pay to live in a civilized society". Researches and advocates for taxes that can build a society and decrease inequity.

Paul Krugman-Unlike a lot of economists, Krugman actively publicizes his political leanings and clearly identifies with the Democratic Party. Much of his work is in the areas of international trade and international finance, whereas his more general-interest writing is more focused on income distribution and public policy.